Original title:
The Poet and the Peony

Copyright © 2025 Creative Arts Management OÜ
All rights reserved.

Author: Evan Hawthorne
ISBN HARDBACK: 978-1-80567-072-8
ISBN PAPERBACK: 978-1-80567-152-7

Rhapsody of Blooming Words.

In a garden full of chatter,
Words frolic, dance, and clatter.
Buds giggle in the sun's embrace,
Poetry blooms in a heartfelt race.

Rhymes tumble like playful bees,
Tickling petals in the breeze.
Each line a petal, bright and bold,
Spilling secrets that never grow old.

Whispers of Color

Crimson blush and golden hue,
Colors have their own debut.
They whisper tales with every sway,
Each shade a story, come what may.

With every shift, a giggle stirs,
Like shy secrets in feathered furs.
Marigolds tease the humble weeds,
While butterflies crack up at their deeds.

Fragrance of Verses

Scented verses waft and swirl,
Like laughter in a summer whirl.
Pungent lines and floral prose,
Tickle our noses as humor flows.

A witty jest in a lilac's grin,
Whiffs of irony under the skin.
Roses throw shade, a pun-derful mess,
As rhymes bloom in the fragrant excess.

Petals in the Breeze

Petals pirouette like a clown,
Tickled by the gentle down.
With every gust, they laugh and spin,
A floral comedy where all win.

Daisies duke it out with wit,
While tulips butt heads in a split.
Nature's giggles fill the air,
As blooms toss jokes without a care.

Petals Drawn to Ink

A flower sighed with ink in hand,
It wrote some lines across the land.
Yet all its prose fell to the ground,
For bees just buzzed, and laughed around.

It tried to rhyme with bee's loud buzz,
But found itself in quite a fuzz.
The daisies giggled, rolled in glee,
While tulips teased with 'come drink tea!'

Lyrical Landscapes of Fleur

The buds all gathered for a show,
In whispers soft, they'd steal the glow.
With petals flared and colors bright,
They danced like mad in morning light.

But when the sun began to fade,
Their humorous plans were quickly made.
They laughed and twirled in evening mist,
While crickets made a waltz for bliss.

Musings from the Flower Bed

In bed of blooms, thoughts sprout with ease,
Where roses chuckle and dandelions tease.
One shouted, 'Life's but a fleeting frolic!'
The others nodded, 'We seem so comic!'

And when the rain began to pour,
They swayed together, singing more.
A daisy winked, 'Let's make a splash!'
And everyone braced for nature's crash!

The Imprint of Floral Dreams

A petal dreamed of great acclaim,
To write a book and make a name.
But ink was spilled; oh, what a mess!
The flowers laughed, 'You're such a stress!'

With every verse a dance did bloom,
And rhymes that burst like loud perfume.
They rolled in laughter, petals flew,
Saying, 'Who knew dreams could smell so blue?'

Love Letters to a Flower

Oh dear bud, with colors so bright,
You dance in the breeze, it's quite a sight.
I write you a note on a leaf so green,
Hoping you whisper, "You're my blooming queen!"

Your fragrance so sweet, it tickles my nose,
With roots in the dirt, you strike quite a pose.
Do you dream of a vase, or of gardens so wide?
Or is it just me, and my wish to confide?

The Art of Nature's Scribe

With petals like pages, I pen my delight,
Each fluttering whisper wears sunlight so bright.
I scribble my thoughts on a breeze passing by,
Wondering if daisies can pull off a tie!

Oh, tulips in tutus, what a sight to behold,
In the dance of the garden, they're brazen and bold.
I chuckle and snicker at seedlings so small,
Who think they can stand like the giants and tall.

Echoes of Spring's Canvas

In vibrant hues, the canvas does bloom,
With echoes of laughter dispelling all gloom.
I paint with my brush made of petals and cheer,
Creating a masterpiece, year after year!

The daisies all giggle, the roses just grin,
As nature's odd tales of wildflowers begin.
I swear that a sunflower winked at me once,
When I stumbled upon a clumsy old dunce!

Petal Poetry Under Moonlight

Beneath the moon's gaze, the blossoms all sway,
Reciting odd verses in their funny way.
The night air is filled with their giggly glee,
As they whisper sweet nothings to the old oak tree.

Lilies in pajamas, a tulip in shades,
Tell tales of mischief and morning parades.
Each petal a stanza, a joke in disguise,
While the stars in the skies share a twinkle and sigh!

Ink Soaked in Dew

With ink that drips like morning mist,
I write of blooms that can't resist.
They dance around with giggles bright,
And sip the sun till pale of night.

Their petals blush in hues so bold,
They share my secrets, never cold.
They whisper tales of dandy dreams,
While sipping tea and plotting schemes.

With every stroke, the laughter swells,
As flowers giggle, and ink repells.
The garden's my most jolly friend,
In every thrum, the joy won't end.

So here's a toast to dew and pens,
To merry blooms and their funny fends.
With laughter blooming like the dew,
I'm inked with joy, how about you?

The Blooms that Speak

In gardens green where whispers grow,
The blossoms chat, their faces glow.
They gossip loud about the bees,
And giggle over gentle breeze.

With petals bright, they tell their tales,
Of silly sprites and misty gales.
They have opinions on the rain,
And call the clouds a silly bane.

They dress up wild for morning sun,
In garbs of gold, they love the fun.
Their laughter fills the leafy air,
With every bloom, a joyous flare.

So if you pause to lend an ear,
You'll find a world of cheer, my dear.
The blooms will speak, just take a chance,
And join their merry, blooming dance!

Petals and Prose

In lines of verse where petals lie,
The rhymes take wing and gently fly.
They swirl like leaves in autumn's breeze,
In gardens where the heart feels free.

Each petal's turn, a story spun,
Of sunbeam races, and frolicking fun.
They craft a sonnet with every sway,
In shades of pink and bright array.

With ink in hand, I write the play,
Where flowers steal the show today.
Their cheerful blooms, a lively cast,
In every line, the joy amassed.

So let us laugh with nature's grace,
With petals soft in this wild place.
In prose and petal, we find our way,
In the merry blooms of the sunny day!

Rhymes of Radiance

In gardens lush where laughter shines,
The petals twirl in joyful lines.
They sing in colors, bold and bright,
With rhymes of radiance taking flight.

They play a game of peekaboo,
With all the critters and the dew.
Each stanza sways like dancing sprout,
And fills the air with giggles loud.

The sun does smile upon their heads,
While bees compose some silly threads.
In every rhyme, there's joy to seek,
As flowers bloom and softly speak.

So let us join this funny spree,
In gardens filled with light and glee.
For in these rhymes of radiant cheer,
We find our joy, we shed our fear!

Dance of the Garden

In the bright garden, blooms sway and spin,
A tulip trip with a daffodil grin.
They twirl in the breeze, what a sight to see,
While the wobbly weeds drink their herbal tea.

A rose starts to laugh with a cheeky bloom,
Telling wild tales of their springtime gloom.
"Watch your petals!" a lily would yell,
As a sunflower flips, shows off quite well.

With daisies as dancers in frocks of white,
They jiggle and giggle until the moonlight.
Each color a joke, oh what fun it seems,
The garden's a stage for the silliest dreams.

A Sonnet in Silk

Oh, a butterfly wears a coat made of silk,
Strutting about with a sway and a milk.
A bumblebee buzzes, tries to keep time,
While roses keep dreaming of love in their rhyme.

The petals gossip like chums at a fair,
"That hibiscus sure thinks it's the best-dressed there!"
But the daisy just chuckles, asks them to chill,
"Next spring, who knows? Maybe I'll thrill."

With laughter like water, they great each bloom,
Drawing bright smiles from the shadowy gloom.
In this frolicsome garden where laughter's the key,
Every petal is humor, so joyous and free.

Secrets among Petals

In a secret world where petals conspire,
Roses tell tales while the sun grows higher.
A cosmos blushes, spills beans in a throng,
While lilacs crack jokes, all afternoon long.

A tulip peers in, plots mischief anew,
"Let's swap our scents, just to confuse the dew!"
The lilies all laugh, their giggles abound,
As the sunflowers nod, keeping humor profound.

They weave in their whispers a dance of delight,
Sharing the laughter that glimmers in light.
In this leafy lounge, silly secrets unfurl,
What a hoot to be part of the floral swirl!

The Language of Flora

In the chatter of petals, a language is brewed,
Where peonies tease and forget to include.
A daffodil quips, sprouting jokes from its stem,
While the roses roll eyes at this cheeky gem.

A vine weaves a tale that's twisted and sly,
"Did you hear about daisies that thought they could fly?"
But their flight was a flop, just a tumble and trip,
As the garden erupted in a fit of laughter's grip.

The florals unite in this comedic display,
Each blossom a bard in their own funny way.
With petals in motion, they dance and they sing,
In this jestful ensemble, oh what joy they bring!

Ode to a Blushing Bloom

In the garden stood a flower,
With a blush that made me cower.
It winked at bees and danced so free,
While I tripped over my own two feet.

Petals soft like velvet dreams,
Tickled by sunshine's playful gleams.
I tried to woo this cheeky sprite,
But it giggled, took flight, out of sight.

Oh, to sip nectar and be so light,
With whimsy in bloom, what a delight!
If only I had such carefree flair,
I'd prance through life without a care.

So here's to blooms of brightest hue,
Who prank and tease the likes of you.
Their laughter lilts on the gentle breeze,
While we mere mortals trip on our knees.

Reflections on Velvet Petals

A bloom with touch so soft and sweet,
Attempts to snag my dancing feet.
It showed off colors, bold and brash,
As I fell into the nearest trash.

In the sunlight it flaunted its show,
While ants rehearsed a funny fro.
I tried to step back with some grace,
But ended up face-first in the place.

Oh, velvety charm, a sweet little tease,
Turning my stroll into an outrageous squeeze.
While you twirl round, all fresh and bright,
I'm tangled in greens, quite the sight!

Yet, I won't grumble; you've made me smile,
With your antics that stretch for a while.
So let's share jokes in this sunny zone,
For laughter best blooms when we're all prone.

Garden of Unwritten Words

In a patch where scents collide,
Words grow wild, and quirks reside.
A daffodil shouts in pure delight,
Making squirrels run in sheer fright.

With thoughts unspoken, whispers bloom,
A rose complains of too much gloom.
It said, 'Why can't I win this game?
I'm quite appealing, not just a name!'

Among the petals, secrets hide,
While worms debate the best time to slide.
Each leaf a tale yet to be spun,
Of laughter, mischief—oh, what fun!

So here's to the garden that brims with cheer,
To talks of foxes we hold dear.
In this place of color and mirth,
We play, we laugh, and find our worth.

Harmonies of Nature

Nature plays in funny notes,
With flowers wearing silly coats.
A poppy sways to a quirky tune,
While bumblebees go 'Zoom, zoom, zoom!'

The daisies have a gossip spree,
Tickled by the wind, just like me.
They gossip about the way I walk,
In their chatty, leafy talk.

With frogs that croak in offbeat rhymes,
And melodies that slow down time.
I joined in, attempting to sing,
But I think that's not my thing!

Yet still, I dance under the sun,
With blooms that cheer and have their fun.
In this symphony of laughter and grace,
Nature's quirks are the warmest embrace.

The Dance of Color and Word

In a garden where colors collide,
Words twirl and jump like a lively tide.
Daisies giggle as they sway,
While tulips whisper jokes all day.

Sunflowers break into silly cheer,
Their sun-kissed faces, oh so dear.
With each petal dance and bow,
They crown the day, take a bow!

Lilies blush, thinking it's spring,
As bees buzz forth, merrily sing.
Chasing rhymes through blooming trails,
They plot mischief in the gales.

In a nook where laughter gleams,
The flowers scheme wild dreams.
For every bud that starts to bloom,
Is a comedic show to consume!

Language of the Garden

In gardens vast where secrets bloom,
Flowers chatter, banishing gloom.
Roses trade tales of love gone wrong,
While daisies giggle, singing their song.

Petunias gossip in hues so bright,
Over a cup of dew at night.
Chrysanthemums plan a garden gala,
While the ferns get lost in the balala.

Lilies laugh at the butterfly's plight,
As she fumbles in a floral flight.
'Oh dear, is that really your nose?',
They beckon her, amid laughter's prose.

In this place where words take root,
Every petal wears a funny suit.
With joy they sway, in breezy tune,
As nature writes a quirky cartoon!

In the Embrace of Softness

In soft embrace, the blooms unite,
Pillowed petals take flight at night.
Fluffy clouds throw a cushiony hug,
While daisies prance, feeling snug.

Tulips whisper sweet nothings loud,
Claiming their charm comes from the crowd.
Sunlight sprinkles laughter above,
Crafting romance, a garden of love.

With each breeze, they spin and twist,
In giggles of nature, none can resist.
A plush performance stars the day,
As blossoms showcase their ballet.

With every fold, a comedy ends,
As petals play, their joy transcends.
In the embrace of softness, we find,
A whimsical world that's sweetly kind!

A Blossom's Serenade

A blossom sings a silly tune,
Underneath the bright round moon.
Petals sway in rhythm and rhyme,
Creating giggles that pierce through time.

In the chorus, bees buzz along,
Joining in the floral song.
With a hop and a skip, they glide,
As flowers cheer, their joy can't hide.

Marigolds paint the scene so bright,
While violets giggle at the sight.
'Oh, watch your stems!' the daisies shout,
In this serenade, laughter's about.

With each note, blooms dance on air,
Tickling petals, what a flair!
A blossom's serenade fills the night,
As nature's fun takes glorious flight!

Stanza of Blooms

In a garden full of cheer,
A flower sneezed, it was quite clear.
The bees buzzed in a frantic dance,
While petals twirled as if in trance.

A spider spun a web of laughs,
Caught in it were two tiny calves.
They mistook it for a trampoline,
And bounced around, slightly obscene.

Daisies giggled, mocking the rose,
Said, "Your fragrance is like old prose!"
While violets blushed in purple fits,
Pretending they know all the sweet wits.

At dusk, the moon joined in the game,
Whispering humor, never the same.
The flowers chuckled, under the sky,
As laughter echoed, oh my oh my!

Verses Beneath Petal Skies

There once was a tulip, bold and bright,
Who loved to dance in the soft moonlight.
It tripped on a daffodil's tiny toe,
And fell face-first, oh what a show!

A sunflower, always so tall and grand,
Decided to boast about his lush land.
But a lilac laughed, saying with glee,
"Down here to the ground is where you'll be!"

A dandy lion played tricks, oh so sly,
Tickling the bees as they hovered by.
The bees dropped nectar, a sticky surprise,
Creating a ruckus that reached the skies.

In the end, though the blooms had a blast,
They learned that their laughter could never last.
But in the garden, joy forever reigns,
In the sun, laughter flows like summer rains.

The Blooming Muse

A petunia wrote with flair and style,
Crafting verses that made folks smile.
But when it rained, oh what a mess,
The ink ran wild, causing distress!

An orchid chimed in, quite the snob,
"Your petals are wilting, oh what a job!"
But a poppy winked, with a cheeky grin,
"At least we're not boring, we make heads spin!"

In a patch of roses, red and sweet,
One asked, "Why do we dance on our feet?"
With laughter replied, a cheery bloom,
"Because when we grow, there's always room!"

As blossoms gathered for a midnight rhyme,
The laughter painted petals, oh so prime.
For in this garden of giggles and glee,
Every rose knows life's best with esprit!

Inked in Blossom

With ink made from nectar and dew,
Petals scribble of mischief, it's true.
A daffodil prank called the butterflies,
"Why don't you land? And witness the lies!"

A lilac painted the sky with its hue,
Said, "I'll bloom if you all will too!"
But a bee buzzed back, quite out of breath,
"You'll bloom too much, you'll meet your own death!"

At the edge of the blossoms, a tulip cried,
"I'm dreaming big, no reason to hide!"
The daisies laughed, they rolled on the floor,
"Take it easy, your dreams are a chore!"

Yet under this folly, a truth did bloom,
In the laughter, they painted away the gloom.
Each whimsy cherished, every jest replete,
In the garden of giggles, life's truly sweet!

The Symphony of Blooms

In a garden of chatter, petals dance,
Bees buzzing tunes in a floral trance.
Worms play the bass, they wiggle and squirm,
While daisies and roses show off their charm.

Tulips are trumpeting loud with delight,
While violets giggle, oh what a sight!
The sun throws confetti, a golden parade,
Even the weeds have their roles to invade.

A sunflower spins tales with a tall, proud stance,
While daffodils burst into laughter, they prance.
Each bloom holds a secret, a joke in its hue,
In this crazy garden, there's always a clue.

So grab a whole handful of petals and cheer,
Join the merry tune of the flowers so near.
The symphony plays, and we dance along,
In the garden of giggles, where all blooms belong.

Secrets Woven in Garden Light

In the hush of the garden, whispers take flight,
A squirrel tells secrets, all playful and bright.
The daisies gossip, the tulips all jest,
Every leaf has a story, a humorous quest.

A snail slips by, slow on a whim,
While chatting with ants, they laugh 'til they swim.
The lilies are posing, as if on a stage,
Each bloom is a comic, with jokes to engage.

Under sunbeams, the shadows do play,
A dance of mischief in a light-hearted way.
With clover and thistle, they share clever puns,
As laughter erupts from the heart of the runs.

So wander through petals, feel joy in your soul,
In this garden of secrets, you'll find your role.
With smiles in the soil, and giggles in bloom,
The light weaves a tapestry of laughter and room.

Dreamlines in the Floral Mist

Through the fog of the morning, the flowers awake,
With dreams on their petals, the bright blooms mistake.
A poppy is yawning, a daisy's in flight,
While orchids share winks, in the soft morning light.

The buttercups laugh, with their cheerful, gold grin,
As a jasmine whispers, 'Let's twirl in a spin!'
A rose rolls its eyes, with a thorny little smirk,
In the mist, they create their own silly quirks.

One bloom starts to snore, with a pollen-filled sigh,
While another retells how the bees often fly.
The garden is buzzing with stories so grand,
As dreams float like petals, all dusted with sand.

So dance in the fog, let your spirit be free,
The floral mist holds a joyous decree.
In this land of sweet laughter, where dreams intertwine,
Each blossom's a joke, every leaf is divine.

Expression in Every Leaf

In the audience of nature, the leaves all applaud,
With laughter that ripples, the garden's facade.
A fern on the edge does a shimmy so fine,
While roses are blushing, with stories of wine.

The lilacs are singing in lavender tones,
As violets chip in with their cleverest tones.
Amidst the green daisies, jokes tumble in rows,
Every leaf has a punchline, the laughter just flows.

The hedgehog rolls by, with a quill-covered grin,
While the hydrangeas laugh, 'What a mess we are in!'
Each shrub has a tale, a comedic little twist,
In the rhythm of nature, no humor is missed.

So gather your friends, in this leafy retreat,
Where the giggles of flowers and leaves gently meet.
In each vibrant hue, in every playful breeze,
Find expression in laughter, and joy with such ease.

Ink and Petal

Inky fingers grasp a stem,
A flower whispers, 'Write for him!'
Petals giggle, swaying free,
'You think you're deep? Just look at me!'

Sunlight dances on their hue,
While bees buzz in and out of view.
'You claim to be the heart's own bard,
But we all know it's quite hard!'

Revelations in the Rosebed

In the garden, secrets told,
Petals blush, and stories unfold.
'You think you've plucked the winning line,
But we prefer our wine divine!'

Bumblebees wear tiny ties,
As ants take bets on poetry pies.
'No sonnets here, just sweet relief,
Come join our revelry, oh grief!'

The Allure of Blossoms

Blossoms strike a pose in spring,
With every sway, their laughter rings.
They'll tell you how to mix and match,
But oh, watch out! They might just hatch!

In a pot of dirt, dreams take flight,
While worms debate if it's day or night.
'You call that art? What a disgrace!
But let's be honest, it's such a chase!'

Serenity in Floral Silence

Quiet buds in the softest light,
Murmuring secrets, out of sight.
'You think it's peace? We just play tricks!
Try holding still while our pollen sticks!'

A sunflower yawns, stretches wide,
While daisies giggle, eyes open wide.
'Serene we are, but don't be fooled,
We bloom with chaos, flower-fueled!'

Imagery of Blooming Dreams

In a garden where giggles grow,
Whimsy dances to and fro.
Petals tiptoe like a clown,
Splashing colors upside down.

Bees are buzzing, taking a chance,
Breaking out in a buzzing dance.
Butterflies wear silly hats,
Waving at the snail who chats.

Sunshine bakes a cake of cream,
Making flowers burst and beam.
Every bloom has a story told,
Wrapped in laughter, soft and bold.

The Palette of Reflection

A painter's brush, a flower's twirl,
Swirling colors give a whirl.
Thorns play tricks, slapping with glee,
While petals blend in a snappy spree.

A tulip's hat is quite absurd,
Whispering secrets, oh so blurred.
Roses giggle at the day,
As they flirt and dance, oh, yay!

In this garden party scene,
Nature acts like it's on screen.
Laughing hues and silly scenes,
Blooming dreams in bright marines.

Flourish and Fables

In a field of wild tales told,
Where flowers whisper of the bold.
A daisy tells a tale of pride,
While daisies dance, they swing wide.

Bumblebees wear tiny suits,
Waltzing through in fancy boots.
Petunias trade tall tales at night,
While moonbeams join in pure delight.

Every bud plays a part,
In this blooming, jesting art.
Fables flourish in the breeze,
As laughter tickles all the leaves.

Blooms and Ballads

Singing flowers sway with ease,
Jasmine croons to the buzzing bees.
A lark joins in with cheeky flair,
As roses blush beyond compare.

Dandelions puff and shout,
Sharing secrets, there's no doubt.
Tulips wear sequins while they sway,
Cracking jokes throughout the day.

Petals flip their little skirts,
Tickling toes and lifting smirks.
In this chorus, blooms unite,
Dancing ballads, pure delight!

Fragments of a Floral Tapestry

In a garden bright, blooms do sway,
Petals gossip about the day.
A daisy tells jokes with a nod,
While tulips blush at a shy little clod.

The rose is a diva, all dressed in red,
Boastful of tales that flowers have wed.
But sunflowers laugh, so tall and proud,
At the bending weeds, both humble and loud.

Think bees are busy? Just try and see,
They're secretly hoarding all the best tea.
As butterflies dance, they giggle and tease,
Plotting a ball with a breeze in the trees.

And underneath the soil's warm embrace,
Worms chuckle as they squiggle and trace.
With roots entwined, they whisper in jest,
In this floral world, we're surely blessed!

Nature's Canvas

In hues of green and dabs of brown,
The flowers wear their joy like a crown.
Petunias parade in their finest attire,
While daisies poke fun, never to tire.

The sun dips low, painting skies in cream,
While crickets rehearse their nightly theme.
Ladybugs laugh, all spots and flares,
As they tell the tales of adventurous pairs.

A daffodil trips, caught in the breeze,
Complains of the bumblebee's picky teas.
But the violets giggle, a mischievous bunch,
As they serve up sweet sap for a syrupy lunch.

On this canvas, playfulness prevails,
Where petals can dance without any trails.
Each blossom and leaf has a story to share,
In this nature-mixed art, find laughter everywhere!

Poetic Heart

With a thump and a flutter, the blooms come alive,
Each petal a heartbeat, in colors they thrive.
A marigold winks, 'Come dance with me,
I promise you'll land on the best cup of tea.'

A forget-me-not snickers, with a sly little grin,
Frogs croak with laughter, while birds tune in.
The humble fern chuckles, pretending it's grand,
While the pansies gossip, hand in hand.

Tulips in a row hold an election so fine,
They vote for the daffodil — its jokes are divine!
While vines twirl in circles, laughing out loud,
Why, nature's great fun, there's no need for a crowd!

As day turns to dusk, with a wink of the light,
The garden's sweet laughter fills the dark night.
In this poetic heart, where silliness thrives,
Joy blooms in abundance, oh how it derives!

Aubade of the Garden's Whisper

In dawn's early blush, flowers stretch wide,
A sleepy rose yawns, a teddy bear's guide.
The lilies giggle, they tickle the sun,
While mushrooms chuckle, 'Oh, what fun!'

As bees start their buzz, they gossip and grin,
Spreading the word in a floral din.
A shy little bud peeks out from the shade,
Saying, 'Oh dear, look what you've made!'

The daisies spin stories of days gone by,
While bumblebees argue who's the best fly.
A chive in the corner says, 'Let's unite!'
And they all burst out laughing, such sheer delight.

In this morning's embrace, let joy take its place,
As petals share secrets with infinite grace.
All things in the garden join in the song,
Here blossoms and bugs, where laughter belongs!

Scribe of Botanical Symphony

With ink made of dew and petals as sheets,
This scribe writes of laughter, where joy grabs the beats.
Where roses recite their witty replies,
And pansies punch lines 'neath bright azure skies.

A sunflower stands proud, wearing shades of cheek,
While daisies engage in a silly sneak peek.
Their giggles ripple through leaves, what fun!
While worms plot a tale of a race with the sun.

A peony whispers, 'Is life just a jest?'
But the violets chime in, 'We're all simply blessed!'
Through petals and roots, the laughter entwined,
In this botanical beat, so wonderfully blind.

As twilight paints stories of color and light,
The blossoms conclude with sweet dreams of the night.
In this symphony of laughter, enjoy the refrain,
For the garden is always a stage for the insane!

Inked in Flora's Grace

In a garden where nonsense grows,
A quill slips into a rose.
It scribbles tales of petals bright,
While bees buzz with sheer delight.

Each bloom a giggle, each stem a jest,
Tickling the soil, what a fun fest!
Worms in bow ties dance in a row,
As daisies smirk, putting on a show.

Blossoms whisper secrets loud,
In this quirky, leafy crowd.
With laughter in every fragrant breeze,
Nature's poetry aims to please!

So grab your ink and join the spree,
Underneath the shady tree.
For in this garden, full of grace,
Life's a joke we can embrace.

The Language of Blooming Souls

Listen closely, dear friend near,
The flowers gossip, oh so clear.
They chirp and chatter, ruffle their leaves,
Spreading laughter like spring's reprieves.

A tulip tells a tale of woe,
About a bee who lost its glow.
With petals wide and colors spun,
They giggle softly, all in fun.

Rosy cheeks and stems so tall,
Join the party, one and all!
With every bud, a punchline waits,
Hilarity blooms at garden gates.

So come along and share the cheer,
Where flowers talk, and laughter's near.
In nature's realm, we find our role,
In the blossoming choir of the soul.

Whispers of Nature's Lyric

In the meadow, giggles rise,
As blossoms share their funny lies.
The violets joke, the lilies tease,
With whispers carried on the breeze.

A daffodil did slip and fall,
A comedic stunt that pleased them all.
While sunflowers proudly strike a pose,
As polka-dotted bugs strike their prose.

From colorful petals, stories flow,
In laughter's boost, the gardens glow.
Nature's humor is quite the draw,
With every spurt of life's grand law.

So stroll with me in this land of cheer,
Where laughter and beauty steer.
In the whispers of petals and greens,
Find joy in all the silly scenes.

Infusion of Color and Verse

With brushes dipped in vibrant hues,
The flowers paint the morning views.
A palette mixed with silly pranks,
In gardens where the laugh-line cranks.

Oh, how the tulips strut and sway,
In a merry, colorful ballet.
And while the violets gossip sweet,
The butterflies move to the beat.

Daisies laugh, their heads held high,
Underneath the bright blue sky.
In every shade, a jest unfolds,
As petals exchange their playful folds.

So come and write in nature's clasp,
With humor held in every gasp.
For life blooms brighter in every verse,
In this funny, floral universe.

Petals Adrift in Time

In a garden where chatter grows,
A flower shared secrets, but who knows?
With a laugh, it waved to a bumblebee,
"What's the buzz? You think we're fancy?"

Tick-tock went the clock on the wall,
While petals plotted a grand floral ball,
"Shall we dance?" whispered a shy little bud,
"Only if you promise to not get too smug!"

Sunlight tickled the dew on a leaf,
The petals giggled in bright disbelief,
"Let's paint the sky with stories untold,
Caution! Colors may run—be bold!"

But as the sunset began to fade,
Our wise bloom chuckled, "Don't be afraid,
With each petal shed, a new tale starts,
And laughter is truly the language of hearts!"

Harmonies in Floral Expressions

In a meadow where flowers compose,
A daisies' quip made a rose strike a pose,
"Can you hear our laughter in the breeze?"
"Only if you stop, dear, with all that tease!"

A sunflower sung a bold high note,
Paired with a lily in a twirling coat,
"Is it a choir, or just you and me?"
"Just let the wind decide, let it be free!"

With each note danced, the petals pranced,
A symphony of joy was forever enhanced,
"Why do we bloom in the daytime bright?"
"So the moon can giggle at our silly flight!"

At dusk, they wrapped up the floral affair,
With smiles and sways in the twilight air,
"Tomorrow we rise, but for now, we snooze,
In dreams full of color, we'll feign our blues!"

Portrait of a Pensive Blossom

A flower sat lost in thought one day,
"Why does my neighbor always sway?"
Pondering deep with petals unfurled,
"Is it the sun or the gossip of the world?"

With a sigh, it gazed at the dazzling sky,
"Maybe I'll try to give laughing a try,
Swaying's not bad; perhaps I'll partake,
But only if I can gracefully shake!"

As the breeze brought stories from gardens afar,
The bloom chuckled, "What a peculiar bazaar,
What's up with weeds pretending to tree?
I see through the ruse—oh, do they think me naïve?"

Yet with each passing moment and chat,
It found joy in the silliness of that,
"Next time I'll join, let me burst through this shell,
Who knew my thoughts were a bloom's wishing well?"

The Palette of Evening Dew

The sky dripped colors like a painter's muse,
And flowers giggled at their dew-drenched shoes,
"What do you call a sunrise in disguise?"
"A cheeky dawn with too-bright eyes!"

Each drop sparkled, igniting their play,
"Catch the glimmers before they stray!"
A daisy dove into a puddle of light,
"Swim with me, quick! Let's escape the night!"

Rainbows were jealous of this colorful spree,
As petals clamored for sweet jubilee,
"Why do flowers laugh with such delight?"
"Because we bloom best beneath the moonlight!"

As the sun dipped low and the day took a bow,
The flowers twirled, kicked up dust with a wow,
"The palette grows richer with every new hue,
Life's a canvas, and we paint it askew!"

Tales of Fragrance and Ink

In a garden where blossoms wink,
A flower's scent mixed with ink.
The quill took flight on the breeze,
As bees buzzed tunes, aiming to please.

Petals whispered secrets aloud,
While poets danced, feeling proud.
Ink spilled like laughter so sweet,
Nature and art in whimsical feat.

A rooster joined in, what a sight,
With daffodils swaying in delight.
'I've written a sonnet, oh my!'
Said the flower while passing by.

So amid the blooms, a ruckus did bloom,
With chuckles and rhymes in every room.
The scent of mischief filled the air,
As petals twirled, without a care.

The Petal's Silent Song

In the stillness, petals grin,
Sipping sunlight, oh what a sin!
A wink from the rose, with a hint of jest,
Kicking back, feeling quite blessed.

Daisies giggled, low and hushed,
While rhododendrons felt quite flushed.
'Who needs a tune when you have this?'
The blooms all chortled, a fragrant bliss.

An owl paused, quite confused,
Trying to reckon friendships amused.
He hooted once, then hooted twice,
As flowers swayed, oh how nice!

They painted the air with laughter sweet,
While zephyrs danced, moving their feet.
In their silence, a song did bloom,
With whimsical charm in nature's room.

Luminescence in Foliage Verse

Beneath the leaves, where shadows play,
A glowbug held a lively sway.
Blossoms turned to light, oh what fun,
As poets twirled beneath the sun.

Laughter echoed through the trees,
With petals singing in the breeze.
A spider wove words like silk,
Mixing verses with morning's milk.

In the mist, a daisy cut in line,
Declared, 'This stanza is purely divine!'
Lilies chimed in with quick quips,
While winking willows flipped their scripts.

Bright colors flashing, a merry dance,
Joyful blooms lost in a trance.
As ink spilled brightly, with a cheer,
Nature's verses echoed, oh so clear.

Threads of Petal and Ink

With threads of color, a tapestry sewn,
Petals crafted a poem of their own.
A dahlia stitched rhymes, bold and bright,
As violets whispered in sheer delight.

Sunflowers laughed with a golden grin,
As a breeze carried chuckles on a whim.
'Ink's overrated, let's just paint!'
Said the marigold, feeling quite quaint.

Together they twirled, a circus of blooms,
Creating a world where laughter looms.
With vines intertwining in jest,
Each flower claimed to be the best.

So gather 'round, let stories unfurl,
Where petals unite in a dance, a whirl.
In gardens where humor and artistry blend,
The threads of creation, on joy depend.

Pastels Beneath Twilight

In twilight's glow, colors dance and sway,
A painter's palette, brightening the fray.
Flowers giggle with petals so fair,
Whispers of laughter float lightly in air.

A bee buzzes loudly, thinking he's bold,
But stumbles right into a marigold.
A chorus of blooms breaks into a cheer,
"Get back in line, we don't want you here!"

The moon leans in, with a light-hearted grin,
As bumblebees join in a raucous din.
"Hey, friend, watch out! You're dipped too low!"
While daisies snicker—what a show!

Yet in this caper, chaos is sweet,
As petals twirl to the rhythm of feet.
Under the stars, in a silly parade,
A garden's laughter, never to fade.

The Narrative of a Bud

A bud once dreamed of its blossoming fate,
Convinced it would bloom extremely great.
It peered at the world, so lush and so wide,
With grand ambitions to open with pride.

Comically tense, it held in its tears,
As flowering neighbors shared giggles and cheers.
"When will you pop? You're late to the game!"
Said the rowdy tulip with a daring name.

The bud just sighed, feeling quite shy,
"I'm waiting for spring, don't rush, don't ask why!"
But when the time came, it burst with finesse,
Unbeknownst to it, it was a wild mess.

With petals askew and colors askance,
It twirled in the breeze, not missing its chance!
Embracing the laughter, it stood proud and true,
In the garden of giggles, feeling brand new.

A Garden of Rhythmic Beauty

In a garden alive with a carnival hue,
Where dancers of petals twirl just for you.
Each flower has flair, each leaf knows the beat,
They shimmy and shake with delightful retreat.

Lilies do the limbo, all decked in their gowns,
While orchids spin tales, swirling their crowns.
The sun, in the sky, is the DJ tonight,
Playing beats that are zesty, a true pure delight.

The daisies tell jokes, filling all with good cheer,
While wind chimes are giggling, drawing all near.
"Join in the fun! Let your petals unseal!"
Shouted a daffodil, ready to squeal.

So bloomers all jived, in this rhythmic sprawl,
With flowers declaring, "We're having a ball!"
And the garden agreed as it rang out in song,
In a world of pure laughter, where we all belong.

Fragrant Lines of Heartfelt Verse

In a meadow of muses, where blooms intertwine,
Each petal a story, each scent a sweet sign.
The violets chuckle, as roses recite,
"In verses of fragrance, the world feels so right!"

With a wink and a nod, the blooms start to share,
Absurd little tales that float through the air.
Lilacs throw shade, while sweet peas impress,
With rhymes that are silly, but also finesse.

Amidst it all frolics a dandelion knight,
Proclaiming his wisdom with laughter so bright.
"Oh blooms, hear me out! I have tales to impart,
Of the winds that carried me, and stole my heart!"

So petals gathered round, eager to hear,
A booming refrain, filled with giggles and cheer.
In a garden of words, where silliness reigns,
Heartfelt verses burst out, colorful refrains.

Portrait of a Flower

In a garden bright and fair,
A bloom declares, 'Do stop and stare!'
With petals dressed in shades of glee,
It chuckles softly, 'Look at me!'

A bee buzzes in, quite perplexed,
'You think you're cute? Oh, what's next?'
The flower winks with graceful flair,
'I'm here to make the others stare!'

With leaves a-sway and fragrance sweet,
It dances to a springtime beat.
A squirrel rolls by, so unaware,
'This bloom's got moves beyond compare!'

So let the garden craze commence,
With blossoms laughing, here's no pretense!
Who knew a flower could be fun?
In sunny warmth, the laughs are spun!

Rhythms of Spring's Arrival

A crocus peeks from winter's shroud,
Its tiny head is feeling proud.
'Hey, world! It's me, I made it through!'
A robin chirps, 'Oh look, it's you!'

The tulips sway in jazzy lines,
With colors bold, they claim their shrines.
'We dance!' they say, all in a row,
'Let's show the sun how we can glow!'

The daisies giggle by the gate,
'Who knew we'd be so first-rate?'
They twirl and spin, a merry sight,
While bees all buzz, feeling just right.

Oh springtime's here; let's not be shy,
A raucous party, oh me, oh my!
Each flower shines, won't miss a beat,
In rhythms where the sun and blooms compete!

Echoes in the Greenhouse

In a warm house where plants reside,
A cactus boasts of spines with pride.
'You think you're tough?' the fern replies,
'But look at me! I simply rise!'

The orchids gossip, all a-flutter,
'Who needs a gardener? That's just clutter!'
They whip their petals as if to say,
'We bloom as if it's our birthday!'

The tomatoes, ripe, roll in debate,
'We're the tastiest, no time to wait!'
A sprout jumps in, a cheeky sprig,
'But have you seen my leafy gig?'

So echoes ring in the glassy dome,
With flowers flaunting their bloom-filled poem.
What a riot, this leafy talk,
In a greenhouse, where the plants just rock!

A Tapestry of Blooms

In hues of red and hints of pink,
A flower fabric starts to wink.
'I'm quite the pattern!' it beams with pride,
While daisies cheer right by its side.

A sunflower stands, so tall and bright,
'I'm the banner of sunlight!'
It tilts its head to catch the rays,
While little sprouts shout, 'Hey, we'll blaze!'

The pansies giggle, sleek and sly,
'In gardens wide, we'll surely fly!'
They twirl and twist in spring's parade,
In vibrant hues, their laughter made.

With each new blossom, tales are spun,
A tapestry where laughs are run.
In nature's art, a jest unfolds,
With every bloom, a story told!

The Narrative of the Blossoming Heart

In the garden of giggles, blooms hear the call,
A bumblebee stumbles, it trips and it falls.
"Excuse me!" it buzzes, with quite the bold flair,
"I dance for the flowers, don't mind my wild hair!"

The daisies are chuckling, they can't get enough,
As tulips form ranks, dressed in colors so rough.
With laughter contagious, the petals all sway,
They're plotting to prank any passerby stray.

A gardener wanders, his trowel in hand,
While marigolds giggle, they make a grand stand.
"Hurry up now! Don't be slow on your path,
We'll teach you some humor, just follow our laugh!"

The blooms hold a fest, there's snacks made of seeds,
The violets are munching on candy-coated weeds.
With laughter echoing, the day turns to night,
In the garden of comedy, all blooms feel just right.

Splendor Wrapped in Petals

In a world filled with petals, bright and absurd,
Roses whisper secrets, not one goes unheard.
They gossip of blooms in a high-pitched, quick tone,
While sunflowers bob like they've just found a throne.

A daffodil prances, with pompoms galore,
"Watch me! I'm blooming!" it shouts, wanting more.
The violets roll over, they're laughing all day,
"Your dance is a riot, in such a grand way!"

With each passing butterfly, new jokes take flight,
"Do you know why daisies sing through the night?"
They cackle and giggle, oh what a delight,
The blooms laugh so hard, they're all starting to bite.

As midnight approaches, the garden takes pause,
With petals all cozy, they laugh without cause.
A slumber of giggles, a blanket of cheer,
In their splendor of petals, they hold what is dear.

Chords of the Floral Heart

In a meadow of laughter where flowers compose,
A melody blooms that everyone knows.
The lilacs hum softly, a chorus, a tune,
While poppies jump in, saying, "Dance to the moon!"

Bees join the harmony, buzzing along,
With bass notes from daisies, they bloom into song.
"Hey, flower friends, what's our next big play?
Let's prank the old gardener, make him feel gray!"

A rose takes a stand, with flair and with might,
"Let's spin him in circles till day turns to night.
For petals are playful, let's tug on his heart,
In this joyous garden, we play the smart part."

The crickets all chirp, as the stars dot the sky,
In their chords of great laughter, let out a sly sigh.
The blooms toss their heads, in their comedic spree,
In the heart of the flowers, oh what fun to be free!

The Garden's Enchanted Prose

In a patch of pure whimsy, where colors collide,
The blooms craft their stories, with laughter as guide.
A peony giggles, and tells a tall tale,
"Once I was a cactus, with spikes to impale!"

The geranium chimed in, with a wink of delight,
"Don't listen to her! Don't believe in the fright!"
As the tulips erupted in a fit of good cheer,
"Cacti in flowers? Oh no, it's too queer!"

Each blossom a bard, with tales to be told,
They speak of the sunshine, the rain, and the bold.
With petals like pages, their laughter's the ink,
In the garden of prose, joy's birth is the link.

"Come sit by our roots, let's share all our dreams,
In this enchanted garden, nothing's as it seems!
We'll spin you a yarn full of folly and grace,
For laughter's the magic that blooms in this space."

Threads of Love in Petal Form

In gardens where the petals swirl,
A love-struck bee begins to twirl.
He buzzes loud with sweet delight,
As flowers giggle in the light.

A buttercup once made a tease,
"Dare dance with me upon the breeze?"
But daisies laughed—oh, such a sight!
They knew the bee couldn't take flight.

With fragrant scents, they start to plot,
A dance-off challenge, oh why not?
They promise pollen as the prize,
And watch the folly through their eyes.

So tangled in the game of bloom,
They spin around, embracing gloom.
But who knew love could be this fun,
With floral joy, the day was won!

Tales from a Floral Heart

Once a rose had quite the chat,
With lavender, she'd sit and spat.
"You're too fragrant, can't you see?"
"And you're just prickly! Let it be!"

A tulip chimed, "Why all the fight?
We should be dancing in the light!
A flower duel? Oh, what a bore,
Let's sip some dew and laugh some more!"

So they made peace beneath the sun,
Exchanged their tales, had so much fun.
With petals fluffed, they filled the air,
With stories best shared with flair!

As daisies joined, the laughter grew,
With every shade, each vibrant hue.
In a world where blooms can jest,
The heart of flora knows the best!

Ode to a Fiery Bloom

Oh, fiery bloom with vivid hue,
Your colors spark like morning dew.
Yet here you sit, too proud to sway,
In hopes a passing bee will stay.

You boast of beauty, flaunt so bright,
Yet miss the dance of pure delight.
While violets chuckle, roll their eyes,
And call you out on your disguise.

"Join us, dear, and shake your stem,
Let's dance beneath this floral gem!"
But fiery bloom just flicks her leaf,
"Who needs your fun? I hold belief!"

Yet as the winds begin to blow,
She twirls, then blushes—oh, so slow!
And in that moment, learns the thrill,
That laughter's what makes hearts fulfill!

Sonnet Among the Blossoms

In sunshine's glow, the blossoms play,
A fragrant band that loves to sway.
The violets joke, with laughter bright,
While lilies puff with all their might.

"Come challenge us in this ballet,
With petals soft, we'll steal the day!"
The tulips twirl, their colors clash,
Each flower in a vibrant splash.

But roses sigh, "We're in the shade,
For competition's just a charade!"
Yet when a breeze brings forth a cheer,
They join the dance, erasing fear.

Among the blooms, joy takes its flight,
In playful jests, they love the night.
For in this garden, fun's the norm,
Where every petal takes its form!

The Brush of Nature's Palette

With each stroke, the colors clash,
A swirl of blooms in a vibrant splash.
The daisies giggle, the roses pout,
While sunflowers dance, twirling about.

The lily slips in with a graceful glide,
"Am I the star?" it asks with pride.
But tulips tease, 'You're just a bloom,'
As petals flutter, filling the room.

Oh, what a mess, this garden spree,
A riot of hues from A to Z.
With paintbrush tails and laughter bright,
Nature's palette is pure delight!

Watch out, the weeds start to creep,
They sneak around while flowers sleep.
But with a laugh, they make it clear,
"It's party time! Let's bring the cheer!"

Secrets Beneath the Veil

In the garden's shade, whispers roam,
Under blooms like a cozy home.
Roses gossip with a hint of pride,
"Hush now! Don't let the petals slide."

The violets snicker, 'Is that a bug?'
'No, it's just a leaf in a snug hug!'
With butterflies eavesdropping near
Their giggles flutter like they have no fear.

Daisies declare, "We're the best in show,"
But peonies know how to steal the glow.
They blush and sway, with secrets to share,
While tulips hide a joke in their hair.

'What's that? Oh dear, the gardener's here!'
They hush in a flurry, as if in a smear.
But in their hearts, laughter remains,
Secrets, oh secrets, in flowery chains!

Melodies in a Flowerbed

In a flowerbed, a tune takes flight,
Where petals whisper in soft twilight.
The daisies clap in joyous cheer,
While a daffodil takes the lead, oh dear!

"Let's sing a song of sun and rain!"
Cried the violets, teasing the grain.
With bumblebees buzzing as backup band,
Every flower sways, a merry stand.

The roses croon, 'We're the belle of the ball,'
While poppies sway, 'We'll have a ball!'
Underneath the stars, the garden plays,
A symphony of laughter all night and days.

But watch out, the weeds want a role,
With their wild antics, they threaten control.
Yet the blooms know, together they stand,
Creating a melody, a fun-loving band!

Reflections on a Petal's Edge

A petal shines with morning glow,
Reflecting all the things it knows.
"Hey there, splashes of dew so bright,
Let's chat while basking in the light!"

The zinnias giggle—what fun they have,
As tall sunflowers show off their sass.
"If we all tilt, can we touch the sky?"
"Oh no," say the pansies, "We might fly!"

From the daisies' view, such antics unfold,
Where laughter's the treasure more precious than gold.
With petals as shields, they share their jest,
In a world where flowers aim for the best.

But as dusk settles, they wink and tease,
"Tomorrow brings more, if you please!"
With stars as their guides, they gather tight,
Reflections of fun, in the soft moonlight.

www.ingramcontent.com/pod-product-compliance
Lightning Source LLC
Chambersburg PA
CBHW071826160426
43209CB00003B/212